A Tribute to
THE YOUNG AT HEART

RICHARD SCARRY

By Julie Berg

Published by Abdo & Daughters, 4940 Viking Drive, Suite 622, Edina, Minnesota 55435.

Library bound edition distributed by Rockbottom Books, Pentagon Tower, P.O. Box 36036, Minneapolis, Minnesota 55435.

Printed in the United States.

Cover Photo credit Shooting Star
Interior Photo credits Shooting Star, pages 5, 9, 12, 23
            Sygma, pages 16, 19, 31
            Archives, page 7

Edited by Bob Italia

Library of Congress Cataloging-in-Publication Data

Berg, Julie.
     Richard Scarry / Richard Scarry.
         p.   cm. -- (A Tribute to the Young at Heart)
     ISBN 1-56239-358-8 -- ISBN 1-56239-369-3 (Paperback)
     1. Scarry, Richard -- Juvenile literature. 2. Authors, American --20th century--Biography--Juvenile literature. 3. Illustrators --United States--biography--Juvenile literature. 4. Children's literature--Authorship--Juvenile literature. 5. Illustration of books--Juvenile literature. [1. Scarry, Richard. 2. Authors, American. 3. Illustrators.]   I. Title. II. Series.
PS3569.C3247Z57   1994
813'.54--dc20   94-3392
[B]   CIP
                                      AC

TABLE OF CONTENTS

A Scarry World

For millions of children, Richard Scarry's books provide the first word-and-picture representation of the world. Because Scarry portrays the best parts of life, his books represent a world that children fall in love with.

In 1980 alone, Scarry sold over 4 million books worldwide, boosting overall sales past the 60-million mark. Though his books have never received any major book awards, they consistently draw praise from a larger, more critical group—children.

Richard Scarry's books represent a world that
children fall in love with.

A Happy Childhood

Richard Scarry was born in 1920 in Dorchester, Massachusetts, near Boston. He grew up in the 1930s during the Great Depression. At that time, few jobs were available. Many people struggled to make money and provide food for their families. Scarry had a happy childhood because his father owned a small chain of department stores.   Mr. Scarry was able to work when other men and women were losing their jobs. Scarry spent his childhood drawing. On Saturdays his mother often took him to visit the exhibits at the Museum of Fine Arts in Boston.

Scarry disliked school and had a difficult time in high school. It took him five years to graduate. "I couldn't even get into college because I didn't have enough credits," he recalled.

The Museum of Fine Arts in Boston. Richard Scarry
attended many exhibits here as a child.

Becoming an Artist

Pressured by his father, Scarry attended a Boston business school. But he soon dropped out. He had always enjoyed drawing and was eventually accepted at the School of the Museum of Fine Arts.

The bombing of Pearl Harbor by the Japanese on December 7, 1941, marked the United States's entrance into World War II. It also sent Scarry into the armed services. "I had a bit of a problem getting in," he said. "Because I wore glasses, they wouldn't accept me as a volunteer but preferred to draft me instead."

Scarry was originally scheduled to become a radio repairman. But he soon secured a place at an officer candidate school. After he graduated from the school, Scarry served as art director for the troops in North Africa and Italy. He drew maps and designed graphics for the Army.

This illustration is from *The Busy World of Richard Scarry*.

Patsy

After the war, Scarry headed for New York City and planned a career as a commercial artist. But in 1946, he completed illustrations for a children's book titled *The Boss of the Barnyard.* It was published by Golden Press. Because the book was a mild success, Scarry was ensured a steady flow of work.

Scarry illustrated other children's books. He also met Patsy Murphy, a Canadian who wrote commercials for the "Ozzie and Harriet" radio show. They married in 1949 and moved to a farm in Ridgefield, Connecticut.

The Best Word Book Ever

One day, Scarry decided to create his own stories and characters as well as illustrations. His first success was *Richard Scarry's Best Word Book Ever* (1963). The book was filled with colorful illustrations and pages of information. It contained more than 1,400 defined and illustrated objects.

At the time, many children's books had illustrations of white children and adults. But Scarry used humorous animals in his illustrations. He avoided representing only one group of people. Scarry's books appealed to everyone.

Richard Scarry liked to use humorous animal
characters in his illustrations.

Storybook Dictionary

Scarry published his *Storybook Dictionary* in 1966. He created a cast of about 70 characters who appeared in numerous actions throughout the pages of this large-sized book. About 700 nouns, adjectives, verbs, and conjunctions were included. Each was explained through action sentences and pictures rather than through definitions in the usual dictionary sense.

All the drawings were in bright colors. They delighted children who loved books filled with small pictures. Each story was contained within one or two sentences. An illustration showed a single word or group of words. Children had more hours of enjoyment from Scarry's book because they wanted to look through the book again and again.

With a cast of characters that included Pickles Pig (who opened the refrigerator door so often that he caught a cold), Big Hilda the Hippo, and Brambles the Warthog (who was constantly grooming his impossible hair), Scarry brought words to life.

What Do People Do All Day?

Richard Scarry's What Do People Do All Day? was published in 1968. It was full of cute, busy details. The book was large and joyous. The multilayered pictures lured the reader into hours of fun.

Captain Salty, Stitches the Tailor, Daddy Pig, and many others went about their business in Busytown, U.S.A.

The book also covered the activities of postal workers, road builders, bakers, coal miners, sailors, and grocers. It was Scarry at his best. His busy pages, jammed with animals dressed like people who went about doing human tasks, sold steady in bookstores. Parents received much for their money. Scarry gave his readers carefully detailed, fully colored pictures on every page. Children who had not yet learned to read could look through this book and figure out what was going on from the pictures. Scarry's simple text satisfied short attention spans.

Switzerland

In 1969 the Scarrys moved to a mountain chalet in Gstaad, Switzerland. They made the decision to move after a ski trip. The Scarrys loved to ski and were enchanted by the Alps. "It was the usual 21-day excursion," Scarry said.

Richard Scarry in front of his chalet-style
home in Gstaad, Switzerland.

"But coming home, we had to pass through Lausanne in order to catch our plane from Geneva. From the train window, I caught a glimpse of a child throwing a snowball—just that, nothing more—and I thought, 'Now is the time to move to Switzerland.' "

Scarry had hoped to one day live in Europe. But his son, Richard Jr., had always been in school. In 1969 Richard was 15 years old, and the time seemed right. "We settled our affairs and leased a house," Scarry said. "With little more than the clothes on our backs, we moved to [Gstaad]."

Besides the chalet, the Scarrys rented an apartment where they stored books and illustrations.

Scarry Success

In 1973 Random House published two of Scarry's most successful books, *Richard Scarry's Please & Thank You* and *Richard Scarry's Find Your ABC's.*

By 1980, Scarry had 106 books in print. They were translated into 28 languages and sold worldwide.

Scarry's books are sturdy and oversized. They often contain 100 brightly illustrated pages. They charm and inform adults as well as children, and they are inexpensive.

The publisher often suggested the idea for a Scarry book. "I speak with an editor who says, 'We'd like a counting book,' " Scarry explained.

"I could say no, but I usually go along if they feel there's a certain need."

Richard Scarry with his big *Pop-up!* book at his home in Gstaad, Switzerland.

Scarry's ideas may not have always been original, but his illustrations certainly were. He created more unforgettable humanlike characters such as Lowly Worm, Baron von Crow, and Cous Cous the Algerian detective. Each character endures accident-prone adventures.

Each year, the Scarrys returned to the United States for one month to promote books, T-shirts, furniture, and toys. Patsy wrote children's books of her own, which she sent to New York to be illustrated. The Scarry's son even published his first children's book, *Steam Train Journey.*

Animals, Animals

What makes Richard Scarry so popular? Many think it is his animals-only formula. Children enjoy Scarry's fanciful pictures of animals more than illustrations of boys and girls. He has also created a wide range of heroes such as Able Baker Charlie, a field mouse pastry chef, and King Coal, a gold miner.

"I like to draw animals, " Scarry once said. "And I think that children can identify more closely with pictures of animals than they can with pictures of another child. They see an illustration of a blond girl or a dark-haired boy who they know is somebody other than themselves, and competition creeps in."

With imagination, Scarry insists, children can easily identify with an anteater who is a painter or a goat who is a Native American or a honey-bear schoolteacher, like the one in *Great Big Schoolhouse.*

"What I'm showing is something close to the truth," Scarry added. "The animals are based on human beings and they'd be living a realistic life. But as animals, they're funny and interesting."

Lowly Worm is a good example of Scarry's personable characters. An amazingly talented creature, Lowly pops up on numerous pages of Scarry's books.

Despite his lowly status in Busytown, Lowly often saves the day. If someone is drowning or if a passenger train is headed for a derailment, it's Lowly who crawls to the rescue as fast as he can. He has unlimited energy in a sometimes confusing big folks world—an experience that children know well.

Scarry's drawings often spread across two oversized pages. They offer children a big picture of rural or urban activity.

Richard Scarry's animal characters take on a human quality.

The opening pages of *Richard Scarry's What Do People Do All Day?* portray a spacious street with characters busy at work. They show everything from a pig car salesperson with a rabbit customer to an owl optician fitting eyeglasses on a cat.

Information, Please

The information contained in Scarry's books also shows exactly how different machines work, how houses are constructed, and how sewage systems work. Everything is labeled for easy comprehension. "Children learn from a story," Scarry said. "And they grow attached to it. That's why they usually want it read to them night after night—and I think it's important that parents enjoy it as well."

Scarry Criticism

Slapstick humor is comedy that features horseplay. That kind of humor is a strong element in Scarry's books. He believes his animal characters allow him opportunities for humor that human characters wouldn't. Characters like Ali Cat, Wild Bill Hiccup, and Pepe le Gangstair have an enduring appeal with their accident-prone antics.

"You walk down the street anywhere and see so many crazy things happen to people," he said. "This is what happens in my books, only more so. If I were using illustrations of people, I don't know if I could put them in these funny, slapstick situations as easily as I can with animals."

Mr. Frumble is a good example. Frumble is a bumbling pig that can't do anything right.

He puts too much soap in the washing machine. He drives on freshly paved roads. He backs out of his garage without opening the door. While Mr. Frumble and other characters get into all kinds of trouble, no one ever gets hurt.

Some librarians have criticized Scarry for his use of slapstick humor. They say it is a form of violence. They feel his illustrations could be dangerous for young children to see. "They say I include too much violence, but it's not true violence, it's fun," Scarry defended himself. "I have cars pile up and people get into trouble. It's the old banana peel or custard pie in the face. The only thing that really suffers is dignity. Kids love that—and they're right. I don't talk with psychologists, and I don't do testing either."

Another criticism has come from women's groups. They said that Scarry portrayed women in traditional roles like housewives. "Their criticism has been valid in some instances," Scarry said. "And I'm trying to improve my image. But I still like mothers to wear aprons. If a father is washing the dishes, he wears an apron, too."

Big Words

Though Scarry's books have a joyful, simple tone, his use of vocabulary was not always simple. Scarry was not fond of what he called "controlled vocabulary" schemes. "Kids don't talk in controlled vocabulary," he said. Scarry used his pictures to introduce children to as many new words as possible.

After his *Best Word Book Ever* was published, Scarry received an angry letter from a mother. She complained that for the letter "X" Scarry had used the word "xiphias" next to a picture of a xiphias (a kind of swordfish) instead of using "xylophone" for it. The word had caused a great stir in her house, she said. No one knew what a xiphias was! They went through a great deal of trouble to find out its meaning.

Scarry was satisfied with the result. "Makes me really happy to think that that woman's kid will go through life till he lives to be ninety or a hundred never forgetting what a xiphias is!" he said, laughing.

Hidden Value

The value of Scarry books is that children of almost any age look at them and are absorbed for hours. Very small children look at the pictures—hundreds of them, as many on one page as other artists use in a whole book. Children learning to read figure out the labels under recognizable pictures of objects—"sand," "car," "rake," "drum," "socks." Older children read the text and follow the diagrams. Or they read the book to their younger brothers and sisters—and enjoy every word of it themselves.

Despite his international fame and success, Scarry was a hard working artist and writer. "In a sense, they are like comic books, but in a different format," he said. "In most of my books, you can follow the pictures one after another, basically the same as you would a comic strip. Although comics is a dirty word to some people, there are very good comic strips and very bad comic strips, just as there are good writing and bad writing."

A Sad Ending

Scarry's last books, a pop-up series, were published in 1992. "It's a precious thing to be communicating to children, helping them discover the gift of language and thought," Scarry said. "I'm happy to be doing it."

In 1994 the Showtime cable channel launched an animated series called "The Busy World of Richard Scarry." On April 30, 1994, Richard Scarry suffered a fatal heart attack. He died at Saanen hospital in Gstaad, Switzerland. He was 74 years old.

By then, more than 250 of his titles were in print in 30 languages. Seven of the 50 top-selling juvenile books of all time were his creations.

Richard Scarry with his wife of many years, Patsy, in front of their home in Gstaad, Switzerland.

Scarry's Gift

Richard Scarry was one of the world's bestselling superstars of children's literature. The skillful blend of education and entertainment found in his books made them appealing to children and their parents. Even more, they bubbled with humor and activity while containing words of wisdom. Scarry's books are a wonderful combination of entertainment and instruction. They occupy a unique place in the learning-to-read process.